BERLIN

Everyman CityMap Guides

CONTENTS

Welcome to Berlin!
This opening fold-out contains a general 6
large districts discussed in this guide, and 4 pages of valuable information, handy
tips and useful addresses.

Discover Berlin through 6 districts and 6 maps

A Unter den Linden / Friedrichstadt / Museumsinsel
B Scheunenviertel / Prenzlauer Berg
C Alexanderplatz / Nikolaiviertel / Friedrichshain
D Kreuzberg
E Tiergarten / Potsdamer Platz / Schöneberg
F Kurfürstendamm / Charlottenburg

For each district there is a double-page of addresses (restaurants – listed in
descending order of price – pubs, bars, music venues and shops) followed by a
fold-out map for the relevant area with the essential places to see (indicated on
the map by a star ★). These places are by no means all that Berlin has to offer
but to us they are unmissable. The grid-referencing system (**A** B2) makes it easy
for you to pinpoint addresses quickly on the map.

Transport and hotels in Berlin
The last fold-out consists of a transport map and 4 pages of practical information
that include a selection of hotels.

Thematic index
Lists all the sites and addresses featured in this guide.

MUSEUMS OF ART

Museumsinsel (**A** D2)
Greco-Latin and Near-Eastern antiquities.
Charlottenburg(**F** A1)
Egyptian Antiquities and 19th and 20th-century art.
Kulturforum (**E** C4)
Painting and decorative arts (13th century–present)
Dahlem Museumszentrum
→ *Lansstr., U-bahn Dahlem Dorf. Tel. 830 14 38. Tue-Fri 10am–6pm (11am Sat-Sun)*
Ethnography and extra-European art.
Brücke Museum
→ *Bussardsteig 9, bus 115 Tel. 831 20 29 Wed-Mon 11am–5pm*
Expressionist painting.

KULTURFORUM

FRESCOS ON THE WALL AT THE EAST SIDE GALLERY

SCARRED BERLIN

Façades condemned since 1945, and rebuilt historic buildings.
Gedächtniskirche (**F** E3)
Truncated bell tower.
Anhalter Bahnhof (**D** A2)
Ruined station.

DIVIDED BERLIN

The division begun in 194 was complete by 1961.
Die Mauer (the Wall)
Bernauer Strasse(**B** B2)
Fragment and monumen
East Side Gallery (**C** D4)
Immense fresco.
Potsdamer Platz (**E** D4)
Small fragment near the former no-man's-land.
Checkpoint Charlie (**D** B
Museum of the Wall.
BRD
Capitalist West Germany inhabited by the 'Wessi:
Ku'Damm (**F** E4)
The stores of the former city center in West Berli
DDR
Communist East Germar inhabited by the 'Ossis'
Alexanderplatz (**C** A2)
The concrete blocks surrounding East Berlin massive square.

BERLIN REBUILT

After World War 2 architects had work to c
Karl-Marx Allee (**C** E3)
Henselmann.
Hansaviertel (**E** A2)
Gropius, Niemeyer.
Kulturforum (**E** C4)
Scharoun, Mies van der Rohe, Hilmer, Satler.
Potsdamer Platz (**E** D4)
Jahn, Piano, Kohlbecke
Friedrichstrasse (**A** C4)
Nouvel, Pei, Ungers.
Regierungsviertel (**E** D
Foster, Schultes...

→ Tel. 20 90 55 55
Information line for the major museums.
Opening hours
Opening times vary. Usually closed Tue, Dec 24-25 and Dec 31-Jan 1. Late opening on Thu (until 10pm) in some museums.
3-Tage Karte
→ *On sale in all participating museums. Price 8.20 € (concessions 4.10 €)*
Transferable ticket valid for three days for admission to over 60 museums, including the largest ones.

SHOPPING

Opening hours
Usually Mon-Fri 10am–6pm/8pm; Sat 10am–4pm. Almost all of East Berlin is closed on Dec 24-25 and Dec 31-Jan 1.
Evenings and weekends
Railroad stations and gas stations
Mini-markets open daily 9am–10pm
Spätkauf
Grocery stores open at night, until midnight or later, and often on Sun.
Department stores
KaDeWe (**F** F4)
The German Harrods, or the store that has everything.
Galeries Lafayette (**A** C4)
→ *Französischestr. 23 Tel. 20 94 80 / Mon-Fri 9.30am–8pm; Sat 9am–4pm*
Luxury ready-to-wear.
Shopping malls
Kaufhof (**C** A2)
→ *Alexanderplatz*
Potsdamerplatz Arkaden (**E** D4)
→ *Potsdamerplatz*
Friedrichstadt Passagen (**A** C4)
→ *Französischestr. 68*
Europa Center (**F** F3)
→ *Breitscheidplatz*
Flea markets
Tiergarten (**E** C3)
→ *Str. des 17. Juni Sat-Sun 11am–5pm*
The biggest.

Am Zeughaus (**A** D2)
→ *Am Kupfergraben Sat-Sun 11am–5pm*
The most attractive: books, records and Eastern European crafts.
Moritzplatz (**D** D2)
→ *Sat-Sun 8am–4pm*
The most typical: mountains of assorted bric-a-brac for antiques lovers.
Winterfeldmarkt (**E** B6)
→ *Winterfeldplatz Wed and Sat 8am–1pm*
The trendiest, right at the center of Schöneberg.

EATING OUT

Customs
In the morning, Berliners have a large *Frühstück* with *Brötchen* slathered in jam, cooked meats and even pickled herring. Then a light meal or snack at noon, and a big dinner in the evening.
Restaurants
Opening hours
→ *noon–3pm, 6–10pm*

CITY PROFILE

- Became the capital of Germany again in 1990
- 3.8 million inhabitants
- 341 square miles ■ 23 districts ■ 150 theaters, 3 opera houses

CLIMATE

- Winter (Nov-March) cold and snowy (32°F)
- Summer (May-Sep) mild and humid (63°F)

STREET NUMBERS

Usually no odd- and even-numbered side of the street: numbering is continuous and 'turns' at the end of the street.

1 Mitte
2 Tiergarten
3 Wedding
4 Prenzenlauerberg
5 Friedrichshain
6 Kreuzberg
7 Schöneberg
8 Wilmersdorf
9 Charlottenburg
10 Spandau
11 Reinickendorf
12 Pankow
13 Weissensee
14 Hohenschönhausen
15 Lichtenberg
16 Marzahn
17 Hellersdorf
18 Köpenick
19 Treptow
20 Neukölln
21 Tempelhof
22 Steglitz
23 Zehlendorf

BERLIN DISTRICTS

EURO €

Check the Euro exchange rate with your bank/travel agent before departure.

VIEWS OF THE CITY

Debis Haus (E D4)
The most modern: from the top of a building in Potsdamer Platz.
Siegessäule (E B3)
The highest: from below the golden wings of Goldelse.
Reichstag (E D2)
From the dome, just above the main hall of the reunified Bundestag.
Funkturm
→ *Hammarskjöldplatz, U-Bahn Kaiserdamm*
Daily 10am–11pm
The furthest west: a view over all of West Berlin.
Fernsehturm (C A2)
The most space-age: from the revolving restaurant, 680 ft above the city.

GREEN SPACES

There are many parks in the center of Berlin. Almost every patch of greenery is dotted with picnics and barbecues in summer.
Tiergarten (E C3)
500 acres of greenery in the heart of Berlin.
Volkspark Friedrichshain (C D1)
The best toboggan run in winter.
Görlitzer Park
→ *Skalitzerstrasse, U-Bahn Görlitzer Bahnhof*
The park in the Turkish district, along the banks of the Landwehrkanal.
Treptower Park
→ *S-Bahn Treptower Park*
A large park in East Berlin, the site of a huge monument to the Russian soldiers killed during World War 2.
Botanischer Garten
→ *Königin-Luise-Str. 6-8, S-Bahn Botanischer Garten*
Tel. 838 50 100
Daily 9am–dusk
A botanical garden with a magnificent 82ft-high glasshouse, and set among 18,000 species of plants.
Forst Grünewald
→ *Southwest of the center*
An immense forest covering the rural district of Berlin.
Wannsee Lake
→ *South of the forest (A 115)*
Miles of beach, with the Peacock Island (Pfaueninsel) and its landscaped gardens at the center of the lake.

SIGHTSEEING WITH A DIFFERENCE

By bus
Ligne 100
→ *Between the Zoologischer Garden and Alexanderplatz.*
Every 10 mins (30 mins, 2 €)
Berlin's most important monuments, (Siegessäule, Unter den Linden, Fernsehturm, etc.) Get on at the Zoo for a seat on the upper deck.
By boat
Many companies provide boat trips through the center or along the Havel.
Tour of the center (A E3)
→ *Schlossbrücke Pier*
Tel. 536 36 00
March-Dec: daily at 10am, 10.50am, noon, 2.50pm
(3 hrs 30 mins, 14.35 €)
Museumsinsel, Tiergarten and Kreuzberg on the Spree and Landwehrkanal.
Toward Potsdam
→ *Wannsee Pier*
Tel. 536 36 00
April 14 – Sep 23: Tue-Sun 11am (2 hrs 40 mins, 7.70 €)
From Wannsee Lake to Werder Island, via the Pfaueninsel and Potsdam.

MUSEUMS

Information
Staatsmuseum zu Berlin

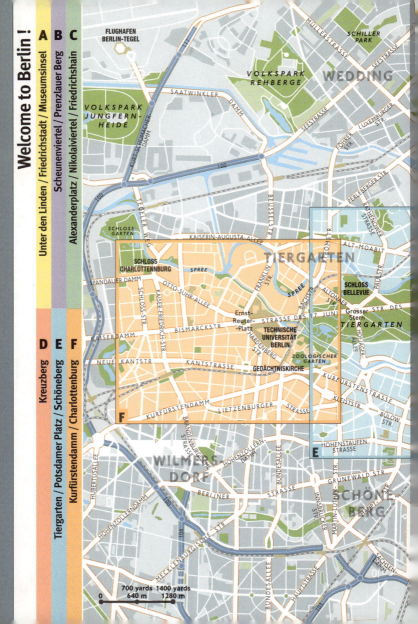

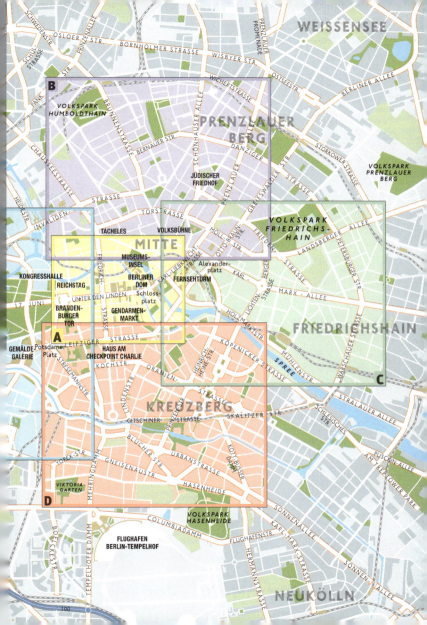

FREDERICK II'S BERLIN

A triumph of baroque and rococo.
Charlottenburg (F A1)
The Royal Apartments.
Bebelplatz (A D3)
Forum Fredericianum and its baroque façades.
Bellevue (E B2)
Palace of the King's brother.
Potsdam
→ S-Bahn 7, then bus 66
Frederick the Great's rococo Versailles.
Neues Palais
→ Tel. 969 42 55
Sat-Wed 9am-12.30pm, 1-5pm (1-3pm Nov-March)
Schloss Sanssouci
→ Tel. 969 42 02
Daily 8.30am-5pm
(9am-4pm Nov-March)

BELLEVUE CASTLE IN THE TIERGARTEN

LOVE PARADE

→ 2nd Sunday in July
Continually under threat of closure, yet growing bigger by the year, this huge annual techno parade, set up in 1989, attracts over 1.5 million ravers.
Parade
→ St. der 17. Juni / 2pm
In the afternoon sunshine, the floats make their way across the Tiergarten through an enormous crowd. Take a snack and a bottle of water with you, although finding a toilet is virtually impossible.
Evening
→ Dans toute la ville
Parties in all the clubs. The most highly-rated are by invitation only (so track yours down in the afternoon).
Information
→ Tel. 252 16 89
www.loveparade.de

Weihnachtsmärkte: Christmas markets.
Silvester (Dec 31): fireworks across the city.

INFORMATION

Berlin-Tourismus-Marketing
→ Tel. 25 00 25
www.btm.de
24-hour information.
Europa Center (F F3)
→ Budapesterstr. Mon-Sat 8am-10pm, Sun 9am-9pm
Brandenburger Tor (A A3)
→ Pariser Platz
Daily 9.30am-6pm

NEWSPAPERS AND MAGAZINES

Berlin Magazine
→ On sale at tourist offices.
In English and German.
Tip and **Zitty**
→ Every two weeks; from newspaper vendors (2.40 and 4.20 €)
Magazines dedicated to Berlin life: movies, clubs, theaters, concerts and useful addresses.
Flyer, Mushroom...
→ Monthly; from bars, clubs and some theaters
Small, free publications listing parties and concerts.

STUDENTS

Student cards
International student card recommended.
Concessions
Concessions available in museums and for some shows (up to 50%).

TELEPHONE

Codes
UK/USA-Berlin
→ dial international code + 49 for Germany + 30 for Berlin + tel. n°
Germany-Berlin
→ (030) + tel. n°
Berlin-UK
→ 00 44 + tel. n° minus zero
Berlin-USA
→ 00 + 1 + tel. n°
Useful numbers
Fire Service
→ Tel. 112
Police
→ Tel. 110

INTERNET

BerlinOnline
→ www.berlin.de
Tourist office website with information in English.
→ www.berlinonline.de
Current affairs, tourism, business and the Tip online.
→ www.zittyonline.de
The Zitty online.
→ www.flyer.de
Clubs and parties.
→ www.smpk.de
The major museums.
Cybercafés
Webtimes (B B4)
→ Chausseestr. 8
Tel. 28 04 98 90
Daily 2pm-midnight
(2.60 €/30 mins, 4.60 €/1 hr)

GAY BERLIN

A large gay community is centered around Prenzlauer Berg, Kreuzberg and particularly Schöneberg.
Information
Manometer
→ Motzstr. 5
Tel. 216 80 08
Mon-Fri 5-10pm; Sat-Sun and public hols 4-10pm
Health, advertisements, addresses and meeting places; Bed & Breakfast places for gays.
Presse
Sergej et Siegessäule
→ Monthly from bars and club (free)
Current events, culture, bars, clubs and parties.

OPEN SPACES AROUND BERLIN

MARX AND ENGELS

FLEA MARKET

vice is included. Leave a tip in big restaurants.

ipe
se bars often have a u ranging from simple wiches to more orate dishes.

iss
se snack bars (vans, or small restaurants) e Curry Wurst, Doner b, falafel, fried noodles pizzas... at a snip.

WS

ervations
n the Internet, by phone, the Theaterkasse, or t from the theaters.
well in advance for the famous venues.
n Ticket (E C5)
tsdamerstr. 96
3 08 82 30
e reservations in on or by telephone.
he day
dskasse

→ In person one hour before the show

Box offices are reopened and a waiting list is operated. Unclaimed tickets are re-sold 30 minutes before the performance.
Hekticket (C A2)
→ Karl-Liebknecht-Str. 12
Tel. 230 99 30
Last-minute tickets: concerts, theater, opera...

BARS AND CLUBS

Opening hours
No closing times in Berlin; the nights are long and the bars stay open until the last customers leave.
Dress
Anything goes in most clubs: the most far-out or trendiest clothes can be seen under the same roof as jeans and T-shirts.
Cost
Prices negotiable for groups. Admission to the clubs is often free after 4am.

CALENDAR OF EVENTS

January
Lange Nacht der Museum: museum night, open until after midnight.
February
Berlinale (2nd and 3rd weeks): international movie festival (Potsdamer Platz).
March
Musik Biennale (2nd week; alternate years): electronic and contemporary music.
April
Osterfest: large Easter markets and concerts in the churches.
May
Demonstrations: (May 1) punk and alternative event (Oranienplatz).
Theatertreffen: festival of German-language drama.
Karneval der Kulturen (three days): multicultural parades (Kreuzberg).
June
Jazz across the Border: jazz

festival (Haus der Kulturen der Welt). Music festival: hundreds of groups and DJs.
Berlin Philharmonie in Waldbühne: major open-air classical concert.
Christopher Street Day: gay march (Ku'Damm).
July
Bach Tage (1st week): Bach concerts all over the city.
Love Parade : see box.
August
Heimatklänge: open-air festival of world music (Tempodrom).
September
Berliner Festwoche: a month of concerts, theater and exhibitions.
Art Forum: international exhibition of modern art (Messehalle).
November
Jazz Fest Berlin: major jazz festival (Haus der Kulturen der Welt). Jüdische Kulturtage: Jewish cultural festival.
December

MUSEUMSINSEL

PERGAMON MUSEUM

ALTES MUSEUM

★ **Brandenburger Tor** (**A** A3)
→ *Pariser Platz*
Built in 1788 by Langhans after the model of the propylaea in Athens, the Brandenburg Gate, a symbol of peace then of German nationalism, ended up in East Germany when the Wall was built. Its reopening on December 22, 1989 made it an emblem of reunification. Pending the completion of restoration work it is being used as an advertising medium.

★ **Unter den Linden** (**A** D3)
Baroque ornamentation (Zeughaus), classical colonnades (Staatsoper, Humboldt Universität), neoclassical pillars (Kronprinzenpalais, Altes Palais) and a Doric portico (Neue Wache, Schinkel's masterpiece) form a guard of honor for the equestrian statue of Frederick the Great (1851).

★ **Gendarmenmarkt** (**A** C4)
→ *Huguenot Museum in the Französischer Dom*
Tel. 229 17 60
Tue-Sun noon–5pm (1.55 €)
Twin domes (Karl von Gonthard, 1785) crown the Deutscher and the Französischer Dom (1701–05) built for the German and French Calvinists. On the revocation of the edict of Nantes, the Huguenots flooded into this new district at the invitation of the Great Elector Frederick William (1640-88), the Calvinist ruler of Lutheran Berlin. The name of the square is derived from the soldiers who were billeted here by the Sergeant King Frederick William I (1713–40) on the site of the present Konzerthaus by Schinkel (1818–21).

★ **Bebelplatz** (**A** D3)
St Hedwig's Cathedral (1747-73) looks like an upturned cup and the baroque curves of the old library (1774-80) like a *Kommode*. Only the Staatsoper reflects the initial pla the Forum that was t dream of Frederick II 86). In the evening, a light glows through a paving stone at the c of the square. Below empty shelves of a li recall the great Nazi *fe* of May 10, 1933 wh 20,000 'anti-German went up in smoke be university's windows

★ **Schinkelmuseur**
→ *Friedrichswerderch Werderstr. Tel. 208 13*
Tue-Wed, Fri-Sun 10am
Thu 10am–10pm (1.55
A master of 19th-cen neoclassicism in Be Karl Friedrich Schink

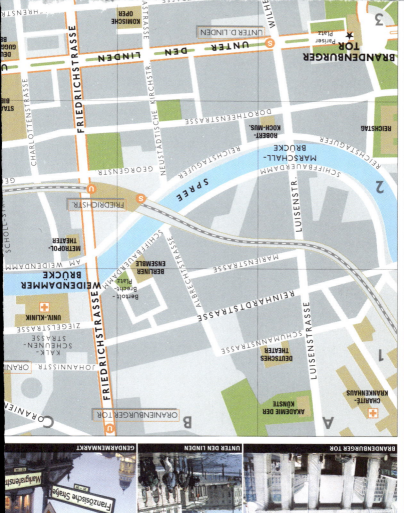

Unter den Linden / Friedrichstadt / Museumsinsel

A

Unter den Linden, in the heart of historical Berlin (Mitte), is gradually being returned to its former splendor. Setting off from the Brandeburg Gate, visitors can take a trip back through two centuries of German monumentalism, from the former Soviet embassy and the contemporary buildings on Friedrichstrasse, to Frederick II's Bebelplatz. Modern, classical or baroque, the majestic façades convey the austere grandeur of the Prussians. At the end of the avenue, opposite the site of the former royal palace, stands the Museumsinsel, the cultural Acropolis of the city which is popularly known as Athens-on-the-Spree.

FRANZÖSISCHER HOF

CAFE C.

RESTAURANTS

Humboldt Universität Mensa (A D3)
➔ Unter den Linden 6
Tel. 20 93 24 25
Mon-Fri 11.15am–2.30pm.
Café: Mon-Thu 8am–7pm, Fri 8am-3pm
The centrally located university refectory serves inexpensive German food. In summer, you can take your tray outside and eat in the grounds.

Suppenbörse (A D2)
➔ Dorotheenstr. 43
Tel. 20 45 59 03
Mon-Fri 11am–6pm,
Sat noon-6.30pm
Soups from India, France Swabia or Hungary. You can choose from six new recipes every day. Take out or eat in. 3.10-4.60 €.

Ständige Vertretung (A B2)
➔ Schiffbauerdamm
Tel. 28 59 87 36
Daily 11am–1am
The photos of *Wessis* (west) politicians on the walls leave no room for doubt: the sympathies of the owner, from Bonn, lie with West Germany. Specialties from the Rhineland (7.70-15.35 €) and Berlin *Buletten* (6.65 €). Beer 2.05 €.

Französischer Hof (A D3)
➔ Jägerstr. 56
Tel. 20 17 71 70
Daily 11am–midnight
Art Nouveau décor, a flurry of waiters choreographed by the headwaiter, and stylish international cuisine: this large Jugendstil restaurant is popular with stylish Berliners who monopolize the terrace in the summer to enjoy the concerts given in front of the Konzerthaus. In the evenings, jazz or *Kabarett* in the piano-bar. Menu 25.60 € (less expensive in the bistro). Beer 2.85 €.

CAFÉS

Cafe C. (A D2)
➔ Georgenstr. 4
Tel. 204 18 13
Daily 9am–midnight
A lively student hangout, this café under the arches of the S-Bahn is decorated in Chagallian colors. Extensive *Getränkekarte* and Berlin cuisine that draws its inspiration from central Europe: *Bortsch* and *Soljanka* (hearty tomato soup with meat 3.10 €). Beer 1.80 €.

Opernpalais (A D3)
➔ Unter den Linden 5
Tel. 20 26 83
Daily 8am–midnight
Smart elderly ladies,

PALAIS

BERLINER ENSEMBLE

FRIEDRICHSTADT PASSAGEN

trendy young Berliners, and women in evening dresses gather beneath the moldings and gilt work of the Prinzessinnen Palace. The terrace is popular for afternoon tea with a cake from the mouthwatering buffet, a Viennese coffee or a drink before the opera. Coffee 2.30 €, beer 2.60 €.

CLASSICAL MUSIC, THEATERS

Staatsoper (A D3)
→ *Unter den Linden*
Tel. 20 35 45 55
www.staatsoper/berlin.org
Mon-Sat 10am–8pm, Sun & public holidays 2–8pm
The oldest opera house in the world, commissioned by Frederick II, was built in 1743 as a classical temple of music. In the rococo auditorium, you can hear operas conducted by Maestro Daniel Barenboïm as well as recitals by the pianist.

Komische Oper (A C3)
→ *Behrenstr. 55-57*
Tel. 20 26 06 66
Mon-Sat 10am–8pm, Sun & public holidays 2–8pm
www.komischeoper.line.de
This is an opera house for everyone: great classics of comic opera and works performed in German.

Konzerthaus (A C4)
→ *Gendarmenmarkt*
Tel. 20 30 92 101
Mon-Fri noon–6pm
www.konzerthaus.de
Hung with chandeliers, Schinkel's auditorium boasts superb acoustics for the prestigious Rundfunk-Symfonie-Orchester and Rundfunkchor. At the rear of the stage, the great organs resound during recitals by the world's leading performers.

Distel (A C2)
→ *Friedrichstr. 101*
Tel. 203 00 00
Mon-Fri noon–6pm
A fusion of song, theater and humor, the Berlin cabaret has, since the early 20th century, been the stronghold of anti-establishment activity and social satire: Distel ('The Thistle') was, during the era of the DDR, one of the few places where you could hear the regime criticized. It is still popular with the *Ossis*.

Berliner Ensemble (A B1)
→ *Bertolt-Brecht-Platz 1*
Tel. 28 40 81 55
Mon-Fri 8am–6pm,
Sat-Sun 11am–6pm
www.berliner-ensemble.de
The theater of Bertolt Brecht, then of Heiner Müller, is run by Claus Peymann. It stages performances of works by the great masters, as well as plays by Shakespeare and contemporary writers. Pre-performance talks are given through a megaphone from the balcony on the façade.

Deutsches Theater (A A1)
→ *Schumannstr. 13a*
Tel. 28 44 12 22
Mon-Fri 11am–6.30pm
Berlin's oldest theater, made famous by Max Reinhardt when he ran it from 1905 to 1932. Today, Thomas Langhof mounts revivals of great international classics.

CLUBS

WMF (A C1)
→ *Ziegelstr. 23*
www.wmfclub.de
Wed–Sun 11pm
This cult club has moved three times since 1990. Beneath giant screens DJs remix drum'n'bass and hip hop for young clubbers. On Thu the turntables are often manned by Jazzanova, one of Berlin's leading trip-hop groups.
5.15-7.70 €, beer 2.05 €.

Kalkscheune (A C1)
→ *Johannisstr. 2*
Tel. 28 39 00 65 Tue–Sun
A vast complex of rooms for diverse events: drama, rock or jazz concerts, tango evenings, dance, techno or disco. 5.15-7.70 €.

SHOPPING

Berlin Story (A B3)
→ *Unter den Linden 10*
Tel. 20 45 38 42
Daily 10am–6pm
Everything connected with Berlin, from key-rings to specialist books. At the rear is a small museum with exhibition panels and two huge models of the classical city and of the royal palace, which has now disappeared.

Friedrichstadt Passagen (A C3)
→ *Friedrichstr. 68 Mon-Fri 10am–8pm, Sat 10am–4pm*
A sumptuous shopping mall. Underground passageways connect the stores (Dom, Hugo Boss, H&M, etc.), separated by several streets, as far as Jean Nouvel's Galeries Lafayette.

Dussmann (A C2)
→ *Friedrichstr. 90*
Tel. 202 50
Mon-Sat 10am–10pm
A large cultural store with a vast selection of books CDs, and videos in German.

Scheunenviertel / Prenzlauer Berg

North of Mitte, the 'Barn district', with its galleries, lofts and bars, has become a fashionable bohemian area since reunification. It is hard to believe that, before World War 2, these restored stucco façades concealed squalid *Mietskasernen*, home to the communities which were then regarded as 'lower classes': the laborers, the crooks and the Jewish community. Further out, Prenzlauer Berg is undergoing massive changes. Renovated buildings stand next to peeling walls that still bear the scars of the fighting in 1945, while bars and alternative arts centers are opening their doors to young people in search of cheap and trendy ways to relax in the evenings.

ORANIENBURGERSTRASSE

PAVILLON

RESTAURANTS

Zach Imbiss (B C3)
→ *Rosenthaler Platz*
Daily 24 hrs
The best kebab joint in Berlin. 1.80 € for a small one (which is actually very big).

Konnopke (B E2)
→ *Schönhauser Allee 44a*
Mon-Sat 4.30am–8pm
The oldest *Curry Wurst* in the city, run by the same family since the 1930s.

Naan (B D2)
→ *Oderberger Str. 49*
Tel. 44 05 84 14
Daily noon–midnight
Simple, tasty, home-cooked cuisine from southern India, best enjoyed with a kashmiri or yogi tea, or an Indian lager. Dishes 3.10-4.60 €.

The Chop Bar (B E1)
→ *Pappelallee 29*
Tel. 44 03 62 76
Tue-Thu, Sun 6–11pm;
Fri-Sat 6pm–midnight
(kitchen 10.30pm)
One of the owners lives in Berlin, the other in Senegal. Together they have set up this trendy Senegalese restaurant. On the walls are interesting African masks and paintings by a young artist from Gambia. Fried sweet potatoes and black beans. Dishes 3.10-4.10 €.

BARS, CONCERTS

Oranienburgerstr.(B B4)
The street for night owls.
Verkehrsberuhigte Ost-Zone
→ *Auguststr. 92*
Daily noon–3pm
For anyone suffering from Ostalgia: Traban seats and souvenirs.

Beth Café
→ *Tucholskystr. 40*
Tel. 281 31 35. Sun-Thu 11am–11pm; Fri 10am–3pm
Kosher food, right beside the synagogue.

Goa Bar
→ *Oranienburgerstr. 50*
Tel. 28 59 84 51
Daily 11am–2am
Check out the pillows in this bar's oriental basement lounge.

Lounge 808
→ *Oranienburgerstr. 42*
Tel. 28 04 67 27
Daily 10am–3am
Great cocktails.

Kapelle (B D3)
→ *Zionskirchplatz 22*
Tel. 44 34 13 00
Daily 9am–3am
This peaceful café has not escaped the passion for all things Latin: exhaustive Brazilian cocktail list (5.10–7.70 €), rum and tapas. Ten types of *Frühstück*. Beer 1.80 €.

Nemo (B D2)
→ *Oderberger Str. 46*

Mon-Sat 6pm–3am;
Sun 11am–3pm
Surrounded by a growing retinue of trendy bars, the *Kapitän Nemo* has held the helm since the Wall came down. Lively conversation, chinking glasses and laughter: a sociable melee that the comic strip paintings, eccentric décor and confusion of irregularly shaped tables fortunately do nothing to subdue.

Wohnzimmer (B E1)
→ *Lettestr. 6*
Daily 5pm–5am
This 'living room' has been in the wars: broken-down couches and armchairs, dilapidated walls and lighting suitable for a blackout. People have been partying here every night for almost three years. Drink your beer at the bar (when there is space). If you want to chill out on the sofas, you need to get here in the afternoon. Beer 2.05 €.

Pavillon (B C3)
→ *Veteranenstr. 9*
Tel. 449 59 73
Daily 10pm–3am (opens at 11am in good weather)
The pavilion in the Volkspark am Weinberg is not just a café and concert venue. On Wed evenings there are political readings (at times biting, always amusing) by the Surf Poeten. Here, people drink more beer than coffee. Beer 2.05 €, readings/concerts 2.55 €.

Schlot Kunstfabrik (B A3)
→ *Chausseestr. 18*
Tel. 448 21 60. Daily 7.30pm
Concerts: 9pm & 11.30pm
A café offering musical entertainment in the basement of a former factory: soft lighting and no more than 20 tables. Modern jazz (Fri–Mon), *Kabarett* (Tue–Thu). Admission 7.70 €.
Beer 1.55 €.

ART CENTERS

Acud (B C3)
→ *Veteranenstr. 21*
Tel. 44 35 94 99
Concerts: daily 10.30pm
Club: daily 10pm
A small-scale Tacheles. Behind the façade covered with former street signs from East Berlin there is art and music on every floor: reggae, bossa or hip hop concerts in the café (2nd floor), theater (3rd floor), gallery (4th floor), art movies (6th floor) and a club (basement). Ideal for getting to know the more alternative residents of the district. Club 7.70 €, beer 2.05 €.

Pfefferberg (B E3)
→ *Schönhauser Allee 176*
Tel. 44 38 31 10
Concerts: daily from 8pm
Clubs: Wed-Sat from 11pm
Studios, *Biergarten*, café-gallery, concert hall and two clubs on the first floor: the Pfefferbank (funky, house) and the unmissable Subground for reggae and ragga fans (depending on the day). Clubs 5.10–15.35 €; beer 2.30 €.

Volksbühne (B D4)
→ *Rosa-Luxemburg-Platz*
Tel. 247 67 72
Daily noon–6pm
This former People's Theater is still avant-garde with a program of modern dance and political theater. The two auditoriums are nothing if not eclectic in their programming: salsa, tango and ballroom dancing (Grüner Salon, Wed–Fri 9pm); readings and songs (Roter Salon). At the weekend both become clubs, sometimes taking over the entire theater. Club 5.10-7.70 €.

Prater (B D2)
→ *Kastanienallee 7-9*
Tel. 448 56 88. Daily 4pm/
Club: Tue-Sat 10.30pm
Pleasant *Biergarten* under the plane trees of a peaceful courtyard; and a slightly pricey *Gaststätte* (restaurant), an annex of the Volksbühne, a club playing house music and, in summer, a puppet theater. Beer 2 €.

Kulturbrauerei (B E2)
→ *Knaackstr. 97*
Tel. 441 92 70
Behind the brick walls of a lavishly restored industrial brewery is an upmarket, trendy complex: theaters, *Kneipen*, galleries, two clubs (packed on Sat) and a multiplex cinema.

SHOPPING

Tribaltools.de (B E2)
→ *Lychener Str. 10*
Tel. 35 10 21 03 Mon-Fri noon–8pm, Sat noon–4pm
www.tribaltools.de
The hub of Berlin's *trance* scene: records (8.20 €) CDs (16.35 €), bags, tribal T-shirts (15–26 €), and DJs mixing music.

Elixier (B E2)
→ *Lychener Str. 5*
Tel. 442 60 57
Mon-Fri noon–8pm;
Sat 11am–4pm
Massage oils, incense and, the star attraction, the Sensatonic aphrodisiac and energizing elixirs.

Alexanderplatz / Nikolaiviertel / Friedrichshain

The 1,200ft-high television tower, a symbol of the former DDR, soars above a patchwork of architectural styles that reflect the successive political stances: the vast perspectives of the Stalinian Karl-Marx-Allee and the modernist buildings on Alexanderplatz stand next to the small studios in the St Nicholas district, which was entirely rebuilt in 1987. To the east, the gaily colored façades of the punk squats in Friedrichshain, with their alternative bars and clubs and low rents, are turning Simon-Dach-Strasse into the new hub of the Berlin *Szene*.

DACHKAMMER

DIE TAGUNG/CU

RESTAURANTS

Mandapam (**C** F4)
→ Krossenerstr. 17
Sun-Thu 6pm–1am;
Fri-Sat 6pm–3am
Modern *Kneipe* with an Indian-style décor, serving a new Hindu vegetarian recipe every day. Original and light. Generous portions 5.60 €.

Nordsee (**C** A2)
→ Spandauer Str. 4
Tel 242 68 81
Daily 10am–9pm
This chain of restaurants specializes in fish from the Baltic: grilled, breaded or poached, but always fresh. Delicious herring sandwiches to go. Dishes around 6.65 €.

Zur letzten Instanz (**C** B3)
→ Waisenstr. 14-16
Tel 242 55 28
Mon-Sat noon–1am;
Sun noon–11pm
The oldest *Kneipe* in Berlin (dating back to 1621) still has the remarkable heated seat on which Napoleon once sat when he lunched here. The restaurant serves a solid traditional style of cuisine: platter of assorted meats (with sauerkraut and *Kartoffeln*), *Kotelett* or *Buletten*. Dishes 15.35€, beer 2.15€.

CAFÉS, BARS

Sonderbar (**C** D1)
→ Käthe-Niederkirchner-Strasse 34. Tel 425 84 94
May-Sep: daily 6pm–4am
Oct-April: daily 8pm–4am
This bar with its crimson décor and 1970s music is so kitsch that it borders on caricature. A laid back atmosphere and friendly, just as laid back, barmen who never lose their cool. Amazing selection of spirits and cocktails (4.60-9.20€). Beer 1.80€.

X-B-Liebig (**C** F2)
→ Liebigstr. 34
Mon-Sat 9pm
The skull and crossbones, red and black flags, punk waiters and revolutionary conversation set the tone of this anarchic, alternative bar in one of the self-managed buildings on Rigaer Strasse. Ladies night on Mondays. Beer 1.05 €.

Astrobar (**C** F4)
→ Simon-Dach-Str. 40
Daily 9pm
Screens straight out of an episode of *Star Trek* and plastic astronauts: a cocktail bar in a space ship. To withstand takeoff you can sink into deep, low seats which make coming back down to earth a little tricky…

TAGSKLUB

NEW YORKER

CHAPATI DESIGN

Cocktails 4.10–5.10 €; beer 1.80 €.

Dachkammer (**C** F4)
→ *Simon-Dach-Str. 39*
Tel 296 18 73
Daily noon–4am
A more peaceful, friendly *Kneipe* for a quiet chat over a drink. A wide selection of teas (1.55 €), all available in low-caffeine varieties. Beer 1.55 €.

Die Tagung/Cube Club (**C** F4)
→ *Wühlischstr. 29*
Tel 292 87 56
Bar: Sun-Thu 7pm–2am/ Fri-Sat 7pm–6am
Club: Thu-Sat 10pm
With the onset of Ostalgia, red flags, busts of Lenin, official portraits and ensigns from the Communist Youth Movements are enjoying renewed popularity in Berlin, sometimes through genuine nostalgia, often in mockery. The Tagung serves Roter Oktober, the beer once drunk by the crack corps of the Red Army (1.80 €). Club in the basement.

CLUBS, CONCERTS

Geburstagsklub (**C** C1)
→ *Am Friedrichshain 33*
Thu-Sat 11pm
At the end of an alley lined with red neon lights, steps lead down into this basement club, once a very well-kept secret. The décor of the two dance floors places the accent on eye-catching lighting effects: psychedelic light shows and illuminated pillars. 5.10–7.70 €, beer 2.30 €.

Fischladen (**C** F2)
→ *Rigaer Str. 83 Café: daily 5pm–3am/Club: Sat 10pm*
It can take over 15 mins to walk through the four tiny rooms of this café-club, packed until 4am: two bars with *destroy* décor, a rather reggae dance floor and another in the cellar which is more of a dance-hall. Last but not least: the minuscule punk bar, where a hip crowd drinks beer, listening to reggae or trash-punk. 2.55 €, beer 1.55 €.

Maria am Ostbahnhof (**C** D4)
→ *Strasse der Pariser Kommune 8-10*
www.clubmaria.de
Wed-Sat 10pm
This is the club for the techno avant-garde. On *Electronica* evenings the dance floor is deserted in favor of the armchairs, but most of the time there is dancing to excellent techno. 5.10–15.35 €.

Deli (**C** C4)
→ *An der Schillingbrücke Sun until 8pm*
Heading from the Ostbahnhof there is a grassy path just before the Schillingbrücke, running along the Spree on the left. Walk past a warehouse until you come to the second door. This is it: an enormous ramshackle hangar decorated with psychedelic motifs for an 'after-techno' experience. Chill out in deep sofas around a massive log fire.

Mühlenstrasse (**C** D4)
Numerous clubs in the warehouses opposite the East Side Gallery.

Ostgut/Panorama Bar
→ *Mühlenstr. 26-30*
Thu-Sat 11pm; Sun 6pm
Very plain décor, techno-metal and a young crowd. 7.70–15.35 €.

Non Tox
→ *Rümmelsburger Platz, Mühlenstr. 12*
Fri-Sat 10pm; Sun 1pm
Décor reminiscent of a building site, rock music and concerts, but a mixed crowd. 3.50–15.50 €.

Razzle Dazzle
→ *Rümmelsburger Platz, Mühlenstr. 12*
Large alternative concert venue: usually rock or punk.

SHOPPING

New Yorker (**C** A2)
→ *Alexanderplatz 2*
Tel 24 72 09 90
Mon-Fri 10am–8pm;
Sat 9.30am–4pm
Major streetwear labels in this trendy ready-to-wear chain: Fishbone, Smog and Raggaza Collection. Ultra-short crop tops (5.10 €), orange skirts, combats (35.80 €) and tribal T-shirts.

Chapati Design (**C** F4)
→ *Simon-Dach-Str. 38*
Tel 29 49 29 36. Mon-Fri 11am–7pm; Sat 11am–5pm
On the left, completely handmade ready-to-wear fashions in a hippie chic style that displays an Indian inspiration: velvet flares (46 €), gold-embroidered shawls (62 €). On the right, crafts imported direct from Azerbaijan and the Maghreb: Persian rugs, kilims and glassware.

Verrutschi/Vertigo (**C** F4)
→ *Simon-Dach-Str. 13*
Tel 25 76 81 68
Mon-Fri noon–7pm;
Sat 11am–4pm
Flowery pants (51 €), ethnic T-shirts (25.50 €) and crafts from North and Central Africa (boxes 21–153 €).

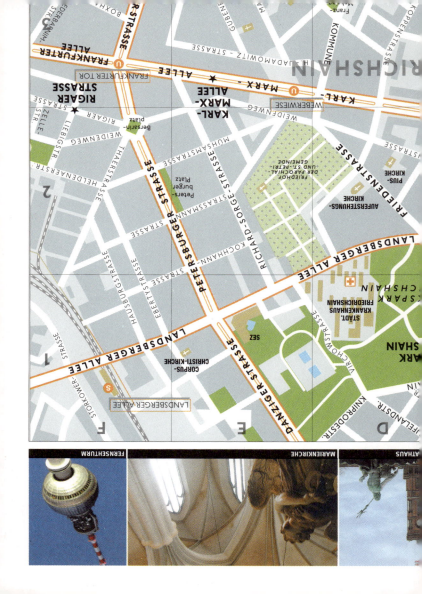

EAST SIDE GALLERY

...efied West Germany dizzy heights. a fabulous view panoramic and the revolving nt housed in the here (666 ft).

anderplatz (**C** A2) its gigantic ons, the 'Alex' ained the true hub Berlin. Completely , the working-class part of Potsdamer de way, in the or an immense de surrounded ete blocks. At the ands the World ck by Erich John, untain of the ips of Peoples.

★ **Volkspark Friedrichshain** (**C** D1)
Behind the neo-baroque Fairy Tale fountain (1913) and its statues taken from Grimm, stretch the woods and grassland of the People's Park (1840). In summer, Berliners flock here to bask in the sun. In winter, the two hills, made from debris from a bombed bunker and local landfill, are used as toboggan runs. This is also the burial place of 200 victims of the 1848 revolution.

★ **Karl-Marx-Allee** (**C** E3)
The asphalt of the former Stalineallee is proof against tanks: the massive parades from the East used to rumble up this colossal avenue to reach Alexanderplatz. The construction of the historicist-Stalinian buildings on this Moscow-on-the-Spree gave rise, on June 17, 1953, to a workers' revolt which was violently put down to prevent it spreading throughout the city.

★ **Rigaer Strasse** (**C** F3)
The gaily colored frescos covering some of the buildings indicate the presence of punk and alternative communities driven out of the center by rising house prices. These former squats, now legitimate, operate as self-managed properties. On the first floor, more or less official bars help to finance maintenance work on the buildings.

★ **East Side Gallery** (**C** D4)
→ Mühlenstr.
www.eastsidegallery.com
Stretching for over 4,265 ft, this is the world's longest outdoor art gallery: in 1990, 106 artists from Berlin and all over the world used the East side of the Wall as a vast blank page. Fresco after fresco has created a cavalcade of colors. Damaged by the weather and by tourists who try desperately to pull away fragments, they are gradually being restored but funds for this are getting short.

KÜNSTLERHAUS BETHANIEN

SCHWULES MUSEUM

RIEHMERS HOFGARTEN

★ Haus am Checkpoint Charlie (D B1)
→ *Friedrichstr. 43-45*
Tel. 253 72 50
Daily 9am–10pm (6.15 €)
On the site of the notorious crossing point between the American and Soviet sectors. This museum opened as early as 1961, shortly after the Wall was erected, aiming at recording events as they took place. It provides a chronological history of the Wall with accounts by defectors and the amazing stratagems some used, successfully, to escape. On the top floor, there is an exhibition on non-violence.

★ Stiftung Topographie des Terrors (D B1)
→ *Niederkirchnerstr.*
Tel. 254 50 90
Daily 10am–8pm
The sinister headquarters of the Third Reich (Gestapo, secret services, Waffen SS) stood on this piece of wasteland until 1945. The foundations of underground cells, uncovered in 1987, now house an exhibition on Nazism and deportation.

★ Martin Gropius Bau (D A1)
→ *Stresemannstr. 110*
Tel. 25 48 60
When building the School of Applied Art (1887–91), Schmiede and Martin Gropius took a leaf out of Schinkel's book: neo-Renaissance eclecticism and graceful decoration (ceramics and mosaics). The building is now used for major exhibitions.

★★ Jüdisches Museum (D C2)
→ *Lindenstr. 9-14*
Tel. 308 785 681
Daily 10am–8pm
The symbolic, 'deconstructivist' structure of this building by Daniel Libeskind (1999), shaped like an exploded Jewish star, attracted hundreds of thousands of visitors well before any exhibitions were mounted here. The focus is on the histo role of Berlin's Jewis community up to its annihilation by the

★ S.O. 36 Viertel
The former 'Süd-Ost the hub of working-c Kreuzberg. The tradi May 1 demonstratio Oranienplatz recalls punk past of this dis The rest of the year, revolves quietly arou markets (Kottbusser and Görlitzer Park), *Imbiss* and Turkish groceries (Oraniens Kottbusser Damm).

★ Künstlerhaus Bethanien (D F2)
→ *Mariannenplatz,*

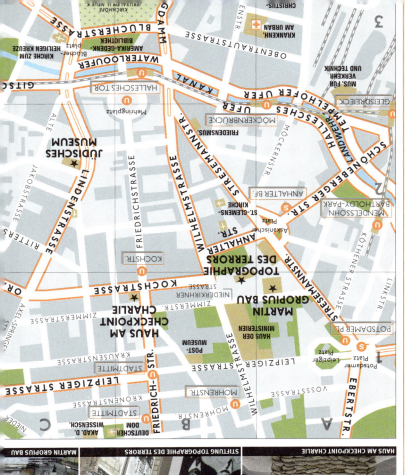

Kreuzberg

Flanked by the Wall on two sides and therefore abandoned by the *Wessis* investors, Kreuzberg was the stamping ground of dropouts, Turkish laborers and young rebels until 1989. Punks and pacifists flocked here from all over West Germany to avoid military service, creating new lifestyles and new types of militant activity in alternative communities. They have now taken refuge in Friedrichshain and, although the area around Kottbusser Tor continues to look like a little Istanbul, the western part of the district is particularly delightful for its ancient façades clustered around Viktoria Park.

AL KALIF

GOLGATHA

RESTAURANTS

Curry 36 (D B3)
→ *Mehringdamm 36*
Mon-Fri 9am–4am; Sat 10am–4am; Sun 11am–3am
A grilled sausage smothered in ketchup and curry: a fantastic Berlin specialty. In a *Brötchen*, with onions (*Zwiebeln*) it makes a tasty snack . 1.25 €.

Oregano (D F2)
→ *Oranienstr. 19a*
Daily 10am–5pm
An original way of preparing the trusty kebab: the meat is browned in a wok with onions, then served with mixed salad in a pancake cooked in a pizza oven. 2.55 €, pizzas 4.10 €.

Al Kalif (D C4)
→ *Bergmannstr. 105*
Tel. 694 47 34
Daily noon–midnight
Take a relaxing break in Palestine: remove your shoes when you go in and stretch out on the comfortable rugs and pillows. Excellent homemade dishes prepared using fresh produce. Couscous, humous and falafel, served with mocha café or cinnamon tea (the restaurant is not licensed). Dishes 7.70 €, tea 0.80 €.

Osteria n° 1 (D A4)
→ *Kreuzbergstr. 71*
Tel. 786 91 62
Daily noon–midnight
You will have numerous opportunities to sample an 'espresso ristretto' in the osterias on Kreuzbergstrasse, Berlin's Little Italy. Attractively presented dishes and generous portions. As a starter, *vitellotonnato* (minced veal in tuna and caper sauce), as a first course, pasta or pizza, and *saltimbocca* to follow. Dishes 5.10–9.70 €.

Austria (D C4)
→ *Bergmannstr. 30*
Tel. 694 44 40
Sep-May: daily 6pm–1am
Jun-Aug: daily 7pm–1am
A traditional Austrian *Gastätte* renowned for the quality of its cooking: *Wienerschnitzel* and *Strudel* of course but also many other specialties. Reservation essential. Dishes 7.65–9.70 €.

Altes Zollhaus (D D3)
→ *Carl-Herz-Ufer 30*
Tel. 692 33 00
Daily 6–11.30pm
One of the best restaurants in Berlin in a half-timbered tavern on the banks of the canal. Light, innovative German cuisine prepared with the best market produce. The

KLAUSE

SAGE CLUB

SPACE HALL

Brandenburg duck fillet with mashed potato and cabbage is delicious. Superb wine list, ranging from ordinary pitchers to bottles of Romanée-Conti. Menu 30–39 €.

BIERGARTEN, CAFÉS

Golgatha (D A4)
→ *Katzbachstr., Viktoriapark (opposite the football pitch). Tel 785 24 52 April-Sep: daily 10–6am*
The Golgatha Biergarten, at the foot of the Kreuzberg, is one of the most famous of the 'beer gardens' that flourish in summer on sidewalks and in parks. On weekends, it becomes a club and a concert venue. Beer 2.55€.

Barcomi's (D C4)
→ *Bergmannstr. 21 Tel. 694 81 38 Mon-Sat 9am–midnight; Sun and public hols 10am–midnight*
An Italian cafeteria-Konditorei: around ten varieties of coffee to drink there or to take out. Homemade brownies, bagels and muffins.

Ankerklause (D F3)
→ *Kottbusserbrücke 1 Tel. 693 56 49 Tue 4pm–5am; Wed-Sun 10–5am*
On the banks of the Landwehrkanal, this white and blue café, resembling a barge, is a pleasant spot in the afternoon. Later, it is crowded with people enjoying pop hits or easy-listening tracks on the jukebox. Beer 1.55 €.

BARS, CONCERTS

Schnabelbar (D E2)
→ *Oranienstr. 31 Tel. 615 35 34 Daily 7pm–3am*
Soft lighting and stylish semi-ethnic, semi-industrial décor: a typical cocktail bar for trendy Kreuzberg. Evenings, DJs play house mixes (Wed, Fri and Sat), hip-hop (Thu) or rock (Mon). Beer 2.05 €, cocktails 4.10-7.70 €.

SO 36 (D F2)
→ *Oranienstr. 199 Daily 9pm / www.so36.de*
One of the most unmissable concert venues and clubs on the Berlin scene. Eclectic programs: hip-hop, ballroom dancing (Sun 5pm), house evenings for lesbians (Wed) or for the inveterate survivors of the weekend (Mon). Admission 5.10–15.35 €; beer 2.55 €.

Junktion Bar (D C4)
→ *Gneisenaustr. 18 www.junction-bar.de Concerts: Sun-Thu 9pm; Fri-Sat 10pm/DJs: Sun-Thu 11.30pm; Fri-Sat 12.30am*
A mecca of black music and the haunt of Berlin's African community. Jazz, blues and Latin music concerts in the small cellar, followed by funk, groove and hip-hop until dawn. Above, in the Jazz Café, there are free concerts. Cellar nightclub: 5.10–15.35 €, beer 2.05 €.

CLUBS

Tresor/Globus (D B1)
→ *Leipzigerstr. 126a www.tresorberlin.de Wed-Sun 11–9am*
The temple of Berlin techno: the leading international DJs perform here. A staircase leads down from the mainly house dance floor of Globus to Tresor: a dank cellar with iron bars for frenzied techno nights. Wed evenings cost 2.55 € and provide a forum for all Berlin's techno addicts. 2.55–15.35 €, beer 2.05 €.

Sage Club (D E1)
→ *Köpenicker Str. 76 Tel. 278 50 52 Thu-Sun 11–6am*
A more exclusive nightclub where faces are (or not) recognised at the door and let in. Bouncers in suits, a VIP lounge, mini-dresses with plunging necklines and designer clothes. This is the place to come for dancing to rock (Thu), groove (Fri) and house (Sat-Sun). It is a club where you come to see and be seen. Admission 5.10–15.35€.

SHOPPING

Space Hall (D C4)
→ *Zossener Str. 33 Tel 694 78 54. Mon-Wed 11am–7pm; Thu-Fri 11am–8pm; Sat 10am-4pm*
This record store devoted to electronic music is a paradise for DJs. The first floor has CDs and a few vinyl records (trip-hop, goa, acid-Jazz). The second floor has a house lounge. You can listen to the music on self-service discmans or MK2s before buying.

Colours (D B4)
→ *Bergmannstr. 102 (at the rear of the courtyard, 2nd floor on the right) Tel 694 33 48 Mon-Wed 11am–7pm; Thu-Fri 11am–8pm; Sat 10am-4pm*
This remarkable second-hand clothes supermarket sells everything, from classic jeans (35 €) to wild psychedelic dresses, mini-skirts and T-shirts (15 €).

Tiergarten / Potsdamer Platz / Schöneberg

Surrounding the Siegessäule and the Schloss Bellevue, now the president's home, the Tiergarten, former hunting preserve of the Hohenzollerns, is a cool oasis of greenery in the city and a popular destination for summer barbecues. Further south, the buildings on the new Potsdamer Platz form an extension of the Kulturforum and serve as a monument to leading contemporary architects. In comparison, the peaceful Schöneberg district appears extremely unassuming. However, appearances can be deceptive: the gay community parties into the early hours of the morning in the many bars and clubs.

SHAYAN

SLUMBERLAND

RESTAURANTS

Goltzstrasse (E B6)
Schöneberg's restaurant-lined street.
Shayan
→ *Goltzstr. 23/Tel. 215 15 47*
Daily 11am–midnight
This restaurant is a must for its welcoming family atmosphere and very good Indo-Iranian cuisine. Dishes 6 €, tea with milk and honey 3 € (pot), beer 2 €.
Indischer Imbiss
→ *Goltzstr. 33*
Tel. 215 49 65 / Sun-Thu noon–1am (Fri-Sat)
This restaurant's kitsch décor has to be seen: incense, a Hindu altar, glitzy statuettes, hangings and garlands of lights. Wholesome food and generous portions. Dishes 5.10 €; beer 2.30 €; lassi 1.55 €.
Tiergartenquelle (E A3)
→ *Bachstr. (under the S-Bahnhof Tiergarten)*
Tel. 392 76 15
Mon-Fri 4pm–2am; Sat-Sun noon–2am
Near Hansaplatz, this friendly, family-run *Kneipe* is located under the arches of the S-Bahnhof Tiergarten. Traditional German cuisine: Nuremberg sauerkraut, escalopes, platter of cooked pork meats. Dishes 5.10 €; beer 1.80 €.
Zum Landwirt (E B6)
→ *Eisenacherstr. 23*
Tel. 218 69 20
Daily from 6pm
A traditional *Kneipe* with rustic décor, an elderly clientele and German or Austrian specialties: *Schweineschnitzel* (pork escalopes) cooked in Viennese or Hungarian style, grills and soups. All dishes are preceded by a salad. Dishes 15.35 €; beer 1.95 €.
Bamberger Reiter (E A6)
→ *Regensburgerstr. 7*
Tel 218 42 82 / Daily 6pm–1am (kitchen 10pm)
This restaurant offers elegant French cuisine, a romantic setting and attentive service: European bass in crystallized shallots with gnocchi in tarragon, fillet of veal on a glazed truffle sauce. Australian wines. Dishes 28.15 €. The bistro serves more reasonably-priced Alsatian cuisine.

CAFÉS, BARS

Café Sidney (E B6)
→ *Winterfeldtplatz 40*
Tel 216 52 53
Daily 9am–2am

NEST 3000 — PHILHARMONIE — DECO ARTS

This large café is popular with the locals: from young trendy gays to grannies who come here for their afternoon tea.

Slumberland (E B6)
→ *Winterfeldtplatz*
Sun-Fri 5pm–2am;
Sat 11am–4am
A café where life is a beach: reggae, zouk and plastic palm trees. This is the ideal spot for sipping a piña colada or a *caipirinha* (4.10–6.15 €), feet resting on fine sand while children make sandpies with beer mats.

Café M (E B6)
→ *Goltzstr. 33*
Tel 216 70 92
Mon-Fri 8am–2am;
Sat-Sun 9am–5am
A lively mixed bar (gay and straight), where regulars and tourists converse to the sound of electronic and jungle music. Order a White Russian, a mojito (4.10–6.65 €) or a beer (2 €).

CONCERTS, THEATER, MOVIES

Philharmonie (E D4)
→ *Herbert-von-Karajan-Str. 1*
Tel. 25488 0 (general info)
Advance sales: Mon-Fri 3–6pm; Sat-Sun 11am–2pm and one hr before evening performance / www.berlin-philharmonic.com
The illustrious Berliner Philharmonisches Orchester make the most of the superb acoustics in the huge amphitheater-shaped auditorium, one of the finest concert halls in the world, designed by Hans Scharoun. There is also chamber music at the Kammermusiksaal.

Grips Theater (E A2)
→ *Altonaer Str. 22 (Hansaplatz)*
Tel. 39 74 74 77
Mon-Fri noon–6pm;
Sat-Sun 11am–5pm
People of all ages pack into this amphitheater-style auditorium. Plays by the Grips company – gentle and biting, politically committed yet good-natured – provide musical thumbnail sketches of Berlin life, such as the legendary *Line 1*, which celebrated its 1000th performance in 2001.

CinemaxX (E D4)
→ *Potsdamer Platz 5*
Tel. 44 31 63 16
With its 19 screens, this multiplex is not at all dwarfed by the Potsdamer Platz. Big-budget Hollywood productions and experimental movies, including some in the original language.

CLUBS, JAZZ

Kumpelnest 3000 (E C5)
→ *Lützowstr. 23*
Tel. 261 69 18
Sun-Thu 11pm–5am;
Fri-Sat 11pm–11am
Ultra-kitsch décor and music: the barman is an expert on the Deutsche Schlager – schmaltzy German songs from the 1970s – and he also knows the 50 most recent winners of the Eurovision Song Contest by heart. The atmosphere is laid-back and the customers (gay and straight) are friendly and easy-going.

Metropol (E B5)
→ *Nollendorfplatz 5*
Tel. 217 36 80
Fri-Sat 11pm–8am
Mega watts of sound and light, four bars, lasers and go-go dancers: the largest discotheque in Berlin is truly Pharaonic, with a sphinx-decorated hall and Egyptian columns... Admission 15 €.

Blue Note Bar (E B5)
→ *Courbièrestr. 13*
Tel. 218 72 48
Tue-Wed; Fri-Sat 8pm–5am
This jazz club and concert venue is stylish and more downbeat. Salsa and Latin music (Tue) and piano-bar (Fri-Sat) until the DJs arrive. 5.10 € (Tue 2.55 €).

SHOPPING

Garage (E B5)
→ *Ahornstr. 2*
Tel. 211 27 60
Mon-Thu 11am–7pm;
Fri 11am–8pm;
Sat 11am–4pm
The cheapest secondhand clothes in the city: this store has everything, although not always the latest fashions. Everything is sold by weight: 7 €/lb.

Deco Arts (E B6)
→ *Motzstr. 6*
Tel. (0173) 617 03 03
Sat 11am–3pm and daily by appointment
Run by a French woman and an Irishman, this store specializes in Art Deco and 1960s-1970s objects: Verner Panton lamps, English sofas (1,278 €), Breuyers armchairs, as well as pretty vases and unusual articles (handbag shaped like a baby crocodile).

Untike Möbel (E B6)
→ *Goltzstr. 49*
Tel. 216 37 19
Mon-Fri 1–7pm;
Sat 10am–3pm
This antiques dealer and restorer has some fine pieces of German antique furniture. He also sells beeswax candles made using traditional methods.

Kurfürstendamm / Charlottenburg

The 'Ku'Damm', at the center of West Berlin, is like a capitalist Unter den Linden. Today, where cabarets and cafés once drew a bohemian crowd in the 1920s, a string of rather characterless buildings houses a variety of shops by the big international fashion names. However, even since the fall of the Wall, droves of tourists and Berliners continue to take the district's main thoroughfares to the shops and theaters. Further west, the middle-class residences of Charlottenburg – small apartment blocks and luxury villas – cluster around the baroque castle and its adjoining museums.

CAFE IM LITERATURHAUS

DEUTSCHE OPER

RESTAURANTS

Jimmy's Diner (**F** C4)
→ *Pariser Str. 41*
Tel. 882 31 41
Daily noon–2am
Dine American style with 1950s décor, rock'n'roll and waitresses in hotpants. Try a Monster Atomic Burger (5.65–7.70 €) served with a mountain of fries and an ice-cold Miller's (2 €). The restaurant uses traditional methods of preparation and fresh products.

Tybrezh/Le Savoie Rire (**F** C3)
→ *Kantstr. 75 Tel 882 54 14*
Daily 9.30am–1am
Patrick Mattei must be mad: for the past 20 years, this Savoyard has been running a Breton bistro in Berlin! Come here for loud conversation, merry laughter and hits by singers Reggiani or Ferré sung by diners at the top of their voices. Excellent wine list and selection of Savoy cheeses. Dishes 10.30 €.

Cafe im haus der Literatur (**F** D4)
→ *Fasanenstr. 23*
Tel 882 54 14
Daily 9.30am–1am
Fine gravel paths winding their way through lawns and banks of flowers, a Jugendstil glasshouse made of wrought iron and staff dressed in white suits with bow-ties: take a peaceful break from the frenetic activity of the Ku'Damm to remember what it was like when people took their time. International cuisine and good wine list. Dishes 10–17.90 €.

CAFÉS, BARS

Kleine Orangerie (**F** A1)
→ *Schloss Charlottenburg*
Tel 322 20 21. Daily 9am–10pm (kitchen 9pm)
Opposite the museums, at the far end of the castle's orangery, an exotic glasshouse and a traditional *Kneipe* for a coffee break (1.90 €), a *Flamkuchen* (8 €), or a *Frühstücksbüfett* (until noon).

Luisen-Bräu (**F** A1)
→ *Luisenplatz 1*
Tel 341 93 88
Sun-Thu 9am–1am;
Fri-Sat 9am–2am
Two impressive copper vats tower above the wooden benches. They are used to brew three excellent draft beers: Weizen (white with hints of fruit and fermenting agents), Hell (strong

MODO

KU'DAMM

KAUFHAUS SCHRILL

wheaty light beer) and Dunckel (full-flavored brown beer). All three are very young and still cloudy. Beer 2.45 €.

Café Hardenberg (F D3)
→ *Hardenbergstr. 10*
Tel 312 26 44
Daily 9am–1am
This café is a popular student hangout. It serves 15 types of tea, green, black or perfumed (pot 3.10 €), ice-creams and snacks. Espresso 1.30 €, beer 2 €.

La Casa del Habano (F E3)
→ *Savoy Hotel, Fasanenstr. 9*
Tel. 31 10 36 46
Daily 11–3am
Wood fittings, club chairs and the heady fragrance of Havanas: the selection of cigars served here is impressive, from the Quintero Puritos (1.50 €) and the Cohiba Piramides (48.60 €), to the Romeo y Julietta, Punch and other Partagas. Good selection of tropical cocktails, excellent champagnes fine whiskies and cognacs. Cocktails 7.70-9.20 €.

Wirtshaus Wubke (F C3)
→ *Schlüterstr. 21*
Tel 31 50 92 17
Daily 11–3am
A small local *Kneipe* frequented by students, artists and regulars who will gladly strike up a conversation at the bar over a schnapps '43' or a draft beer (2.15 €).

THEATER, OPERA, JAZZ, CLUBS

Theater des Westens (F D3)
→ *Kantstr. 12*
Tel. (0180) 599 89 99
Bernhard Sehring's building, a blend of baroque, neoclassicism and Jugendstil (1896), stages all types of revues and musicals for quality theater with mass appeal.

Deutsche Oper (F C2)
→ *Bismarckstr. 35*
Tel. 343 84 55
Tickets: Mon-Sat from 11am to one hour before the show; Sun 10am–2pm
West Berlin's opera house: lavish productions and international stars.

A-Trane (F C3)
→ *Pestalozzistr. 105*
Tel. 313 25 50
Sun-Thu 9pm–2am; Fri-Sat 9pm–6am/Concerts: Mon 9.30pm; Tue-Sun 10pm
Small concert hall for a big club that bills all the top jazz performers but is also keen to promote local talent. 7.70-20.45 €.

Quasimodo (F D3)
→ *Kantstr. 12a*
Tel. 312 80 86
Daily 9pm
Concerts: 10.30pm (advance ticket sales from 5pm)
Under the café is the jazz club, which not only puts on stars, but also holds legendary jam sessions: traditional jazz on Tue, acid jazz and blues on Wed, when the audience is young and the atmosphere charged. Admission 8–21 € (jam sessions 2.55 €).

Abraxas (F C3)
→ *Kantstr. 134*
Tel.312 94 93 Tue-Sun 10pm
A paradise of Latin music: Latin jazz, salsa, samba or bossa with a relaxed atmosphere and talented dancers. Smart dress essential. Admission 5 €.

SHOPPING

KaDeWe (F F4)
→ *Tauentzienstr. 21-24*
Tel. 212 10
Mon-Fri 9.30am–8pm; Sat 9am–4pm
This is the largest store in Europe, dating from 1907. It sells everything, from haute couture to the complete range of Ritter Sport (chocolate bars in extravagant flavors). The food hall boasts over 1000 types of sausage.

Ku'Damm (F E4)
This is the place for prestigious labels.

Prada
→ *Kurfürstendamm 188*
Tel. 884 80 70
Mon-Fri 10am–7pm;
Sat 10am–4pm

Chanel
→ *Fasanenstr. 30*
Tel. 885 14 24
Mon-Fri 10am–7pm;
Sat 10am–4pm

New Steinbruch (F E4)
→ *Kurfürstendamm 237*
Tel. 88 55 21 26
Mon-Fri 10am–8pm;
Sat 10am–4pm
Trendy, stylish fashions: satin pants, T-shirts (15 – 46 €) and high boots for drag queens.

Kaufhaus Schrill (F D4)
→ *Bleibtreustr. 46*
Tel. 882 40 48 Mon-Fri 2–8pm; Sat 11am–4pm
Sequined dresses, fishnet or leopard-skin stockings, wigs and novelty ties: everything for the queen (or king) of the night.

Stilwerk (F C3)
→ *Kantstr .17*
Tel. 31 51 50
Mon-Fri 10am–8pm;
Sat 10am–4pm
A shopping mall dedicated to household goods: leading labels (Conran, Ligne Roset etc.), but also local designers, antique dealers, and even a piano vendor.

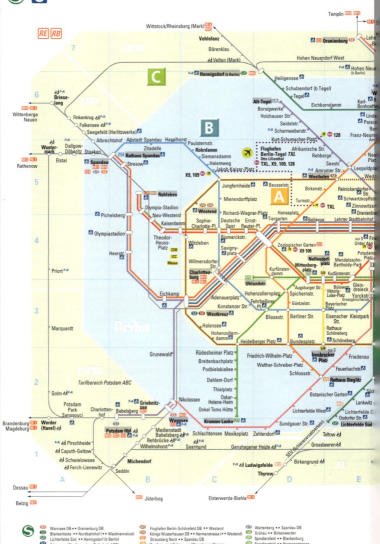

Index thématique

The letters (**A, B, C...**) refer to the matching neighborhood section. Letters on their own refer to the spread with useful addresses (restaurants, bars, shops). Letters followed by a star (**A★**) refer to the spread with a fold-out map and places to visit. The number (**1**) refers to the spread **Welcome to Berlin!**

Imbiss (litt. 'a snack')
Kneipen (German pub)
Biergarten (beer garden)

CUISINE

African
The Chop Bar **B**
Americain
Jimmy's Diner **F**
Austrian
Austria **D**
Zum Landwirt **E**
Fish
Nordsee **C**
French
Bamberger Reiter **E**
Tybrezh/Le Savoie Rire **F**
German
Altes Zollhaus **D**
Kellerrestaurant **B★**
Humboldt Universität Mensa **A**
Kleine Orangerie **F**
Ständige Vertretung **A**
Tiergartenquelle **E**
Zum Landwirt **E**
Zur letzten Instanz **C**
Indian
Indischer Imbiss **E**
Mandapam **C**
Naan **B**
Shayan **E**
International
Fernsehturm **C★**
Französischer Hof **A**
Iranian
Shayan **E**
Italian
Osteria n° 1 **D**
Jewish
Beth Café **B**
Palestinian
Al Kalif **D**
Soups
Suppenbörse **A**

IMBISS

Curry Wurst
Curry 36 **D**
Konnopke **B**
Kebabs
Oregano **D**
Zach Imbiss **B**

BIERGARTEN, CAFÉS

Biergarten
Golgatha **D**
Opernpalais **A**
Pavillon **B**
Pfefferberg **B**
Prater **B**
Cafés
Ankerklause **D**
Barcomi's **B**
Beth Café **B**
Cafe C. **A**
Café Hardenberg **F**
Cafe im Litteraturhaus **F**
Café Sidney **E**
Fernsehturm **C★**
Kapelle **B**
Kleine Orangerie **F**
Opernpalais **A**
Savignyplatz **F★**
Slumberland **E**
Tearoom
Opernpalais **A**

GOING OUT

Brasserie
Luisen-Bräu **F**
Bars, Kneipen
Acud **B**
Ankerklause **D**
Cafe C. **A**
Dachkammer **C**
Die Tagung/Cube Club **C**
Fischladen **C**
Hackesche Höfe **B★**
Jazz Café
see Junktion Bar **D**
Kulturbrauerei **B**
Kumpelnest 3000 **E**
Nemo **B**
Pavillon **B**
Pfefferberg **B**
Savignyplatz **F★**
Schlot Kunstfabrik **B**
Tacheles **B★**
Tiergartenquelle **E**
Verkehrsberuhigte Ost-Zone **E**
Wirtshaus Wubke **F**
Wohnzimmer **B**
X-B-Liebig **C**
Zur letzten Instanz **C**
Cigar bar
La Casa del Habano **F**
Cocktail bars
Astrobar **C**
Café M **E**
Goa Bar **B**
Kapelle **B**
La Casa del Habano **F**
Lounge 808 **B**
Schnabelbar **D**
Slumberland **E**
Sonderbar **C**
Movie theaters
Acud **B**
CinemaxX **E**
Hackesche Höfe **B★**
Kulturbrauerei **B**
Tacheles **B★**
Clubs
Abraxas **F**
Acud **B**
Blue Note Bar **E**
Deli **C**
Die Tagung/Cube Club **C**
Fischladen **C**
Geburstagsklub **C**
Kalkscheune **A**
Kulturbrauerei **B**
Kumpelnest 3000 **E**
Maria am Ostbahnhof **C**
Metropol **E**
Non Tox **C**
Ostgut/Panorama Bar **C**
Pfefferbank see Pfefferberg **B**
Sage Club **D**
SO 36 **D**
Subground see Pfefferberg **B**
Tresor/Globus **D**
Volksbühne **B**
WMF **A**
Concert venues
Acud **B**
Junktion Bar **D**
Kalkscheune **A**
Non Tox **C**
Pavillon **B**
Pfefferberg **B**
Razzle Dazzle **C**
SO 36 **D**
Tacheles **B★**
Volksbühne **B**
Classical concert venues / opera houses
Konzerthaus **A**
Philharmonie **A**
Deutsche Oper **F**
Komische Oper **A**
Staatsoper **A**
Jazz
A-Trane **F**
Blue Note Bar **E**
Junktion Bar **D**
Quasimodo **F**
Schlot Kunstfabrik **B**
Lectures
Pavillon **B**
Theaters
Acud **B**
Berliner Ensemble **A**
Deutsches Theater **A**
Hackesche Höfe **B★**
Kulturbrauerei **B**
Prater **B**
Theater des Westens **F**
Volksbühne **B**